I am Woman:
The Journey Continues...

If you missed it…

Also available by Dr. Joy Lough

Tears of Joy: A Poetic Journey in the Life of Ms. Joy

I am Woman:
The Journey Continues

Dr. Joy Lough

JOY LOUGH
ENTERPRISES

©2015

First Printing: 2015

ISBN 978-0-9960656-0-3

Joy Lough Enterprises, LLC
1183 University Drive #105-125
Burlington, NC 27215

www.joylough.com

Ordering Information:

Special discounts are available on quantity purchases by corporations, associations, educators, and others. For details, contact the publisher at the above listed address.

U.S. trade bookstores and wholesalers: Please contact

Tel: (336) 223-4778 or email info@joylough.com

Dedication

This book is dedicated to YOU - the reader. May your life be
encouraged, enlightened and motivated. ☺

Contents

Acknowledgements..**ix**

Introduction **1**

Chapter 1: The Woman **3**

I am Woman   5
About Me   8
Something we don't talk about   11
Proud to be Me   15
I sit and Wonder   22
Detox   26
I Tried   29
Beautiful   34
Work   36

Chapter 2: The Mother..**38**

That's why I love you   40
That Disease   42
Precious   43

Chapter 3: The Friend..**46**

What is your Voice?   48
What is your song?   51
Listen to my song   54
Metamorphosis   57
Listen to my voice   60
Tears of Joy   62

Chapter 4: To be Continued **64**

Pictures..**67**

Acknowledgements

Thank you, My Heavenly Father, for your mercy and grace. Without you, I know I would not have done anything or been anybody.

Introduction

I am woman provides snapshots of what my life has been as a

single mother, a wife, then a single parent again.

It is now time to experience…

I am Woman!!!!

I am Woman…

Chapter 1: I am Woman

I am Woman…

I am woman

I am woman
I am mother
I am daughter
I am sister
I am friend

I am woman
I am courage
I am wisdom
I am boldness
I am peace
I am phenomenal
I am woman

My heart - as FRAGILE as it is…
Allows me to FORGIVE …
It allows me to love…it allows me to care
And even in disappointment
I am still there
and will smile through it all
You will never know my pain
You will never see my tears
Unless I choose to share with you

My lips speak truth
My lips speak healing
When I speak – you need to listen
To the words that tell stories
That are passed down from generation to generation
I speak words of inspiration
And Words of encouragement
Every word I speak
Is meant to be heard

I am 100% mate to my man...
I am his friend, confident, his voice of reason, financial
manager, his cook, his maid
All in one day
And still make time for some love making
And a little play play -HAAAY!

God allows ME - to carry life
From conception to birth
And then God provided me with
the instinct to nurture and protect
Who else but a woman can make a dollar out of 15 cents?
I am mother and father
So don't even bother
messing with my kids
For my children
I am judge and jury
You need to think twice…
Trust me… it won't be nice
If you cross me…
For my children I am doctor, I am chauffer
I am the disciplinarian and educator
…I have 20/20 vision
With perfect hearing –
Did you catch that?

I am the definition of strength
I am the bond holding the family together
I am the lioness protecting my king and cubs
I am woman

There is a beauty in me that goes beyond physical
It expounds to a personality that exudes
Gentleness, compassion, patience and sincerity
I walk with my head up high
Because I am...

I am Woman…

Confident, but never arrogant
I AM SEXY!

I have enough intelligence to know that God will catch me
when I fall
I know that it is in the journey that I become strong
Knowing that my purpose to stay prayed up
And all my praises must remain turned up

Genesis 2: 22-23 says…And the rib which the Lord God had
taken from man… made he a woman.. and he brought her to
the man.. and Adam said… this is now the bone of my bones
and flesh of my flesh.. she shall be called woman….

That's me
I AM WOMAN!

About me (My Icebreaker Speech for Toastmasters)

My name is Joy
Joy Lough – to be exact…
I was born in Roanoke, Virginia
I am my mother's only child
I had a brother but he passed before I was born –
Growing up was lonely and contrary to what others may say –
being an only child was NOT great…I hated it…

So I had made up my mind to have as many kids as possible –
because I didn't want them to experience the loneliness that I
felt…. but that didn't work out either – a lot of complications
during pregnancy with both of the children that I have been
blessed with.

I have a Son – JaQuavious and Daughter - Ja Quaviyah
Their names mean "Lord protect my child"

So… I am a mother, daughter and a teacher.

I started a nonprofit that focused on musical enrichment to
underprivileged children I teach beginning piano and
beginning theory…

I now teach business classes at various colleges/universities…
I give webinars on Leadership, Communication and
Motivation, Human Resources and Self-esteem

I am also a student – I have a bachelor's in Business
Management from Guilford College with a concentration on
Human Resources Management, an Executive MBA from
Colorado Technical University and my PhD in Organization
and Management from Capella University. My dissertation
topic is on Success Factors for African American
Entrepreneurs in North Carolina. But I never stop learning!

I am Woman…

I am a consultant… My company Joy Lough Enterprises
Our mission is to IMPACT lives personally and professionally
through education, motivation and inspiration.

IMPACT…
Improve
Magnify
Push
And
Challenge your
Thought Process…..

I am excited about my accomplishments but stressed at
Times and ….

So I write and I sing …. Which is one of the reasons I have
continued in my journey - this journey of life that I am sharing
with you. I want to see what the end will bring. I am enjoying
the chapters while learning to appreciate both the good and
bad lessons.

You see…I want to be able to
Captivate my audience and do it effectively
Encourage others to pursue their dreams
Help others understand that it's really not as bad as it seems
And I want to inspire them to succeed
I want to motivate, stimulate, and help them believe in…
Themselves
In spite of what others may say
Or think
Help them find that positive energy
So they can realize that they can be what they want to be

But I can only do this by continuing to speak

Because then and only then will I be able to reach

Them and …
And in turn reach my goals and
Who knows what the future holds for the new
Dr. Joy Lough!

I am Woman…

Something we don't talk about….

My name is Joy Lough and
I once was a victim of domestic violence and
There once was a time when I didn't speak about it
I kept silent
Until I realized that it was my silence
that killed…
It was my silence that enabled another abuser to keep
abusing
It was my silence that allowed the devil to keep confusing
My mind
And every time
I looked around
What I found
Was the opposite of what I was searching for
So I allowed myself to open doors
that should have remained closed
And maybe you don't know
what it is that I have been through…I suppose
There is a possibility that none of this has impacted you
but allow me to share with you…
You see statistics say
Every 9 seconds in the United States
a woman is assaulted or beaten
That means in a minute the number 1 turns to seven
And that equates to someone else not making it to heaven
Because every day in the US
More than three women are murdered by their husbands
or boyfriends.
So I ask you … when will this madness end?
When will we be mindful and take heed to what our
children see
I am sure you know that saying that children learn from
what they see
Did you know that studies suggest that up to 10 million

children witness some form of domestic violence
annually?
That means it could be physically, mentally,
emotionally,
sexually, financially or spiritually
And Domestic violence is the leading cause of injury
to women—more than car accidents, muggings, and
rapes combined.
I hope you don't mind
that I have taken this time
to share with you...
Around the world, at least one in every three women
have been beaten, coerced into sex or otherwise abused
during her lifetime.
And it's not just women ... men are victims too
Studies suggest that as many as 1 in 3 victims are male
And that's the reported cases...so what does that tell
you?
So now...I encourage you to
Learn as much as you can about domestic violence
I encourage you to Break the silence
Talk to someone you suspect is a victim
Let our young people know early that knowledge is
wisdom
And that violence in a relationship is never ok
We have to start acting and speaking in a way
That is positive and supportive
We must work with local domestic violence agencies
that do the same
Understanding this is not a game
And finally... Look beside you, look in front of you...
look behind you
Someone you see...
Someone you know...
Fits one of these statistics
And you can't say that it's not true....

I am Woman…

You looking at me and I'm looking at you…
And I once was that somebody
I am asking you …to help me put an end to this madness…

My name is Joy Lough….I am a survivor of Domestic Violence

Why is this something we don't talk about?

I work with many low income families and many who are African American….I was working with a young black boy one day tutoring piano… just out the blue he says – he didn't like that he was black… He wished he was white….. I was compelled to share this next poem with him….

I am Woman…

PROUD TO BE ME!!

I'm proud to be me
I'm proud of my history
This month of February
This month of getting to know about me
Getting to know the part of me
That some want to be suppress or hold back
They want me to feel a lack
Of worth
Of contribution
Of my understanding
Of the truth
You know what??
It was like they were depriving me of my youth…..
The black history that is taught in schools
Somehow makes me feel like I don't have the tools
To be successful
Why is that?
The black history they try to teach
Consists of only an "I have a dream speech"
And not to take away from the DREAM
But what about all the other things
Why are they
Keeping from me
My true identity?
Trust and believe
I am no fool
I don't put all my trust in those schools
That have goals
To make me NOT know
About me
And my history
My black history
You see my history is so much more
But they try to design it so that I will have the mentality to
remain poor

When it was someone like me
That has made life a little easier for us all to endure
Did your know a man named Lloyd Ray invented the dust pan
And what about William Purvis invented the fountain pen
And what about– TW Stewart and the first mop
I need you all to stop
And think about this…..

It's like Joseph Winters - Like it didn't matter –
They never told me about his invention of the fire escape
ladder
And what about– super bowl Sunday
When you lean back in your recliner
That day would not be the same without Payton Johnson
He reminded us to relax – so why have we been denied this?

My history opened doors
Lee Burridge and Newman Marshan invented the typewriter
Remember there was a time – when we couldn't read or write
Then the words were sent to the press- the printing press
invented by a black man - W.A. Lavalette
They didn't want us to
And that's because they knew
Who we really are
And what about the light
The Light bulb – Lewis Later and Joseph Nichols
Light switch – Granville Woods
The lack of this knowledge
It seems ALL of this was done to suppress me
from learning of my history
Why is that?
What about all the love and care and yes even the bills that
arrive at our home
We can thank Philip Downing for the mail box in front of our
home

I am Woman…

Almost everything you see – is a part of my history
So why didn't they tell me?
These everyday items were invented by someone like me
This is a major part my history
Again…I ask why didn't they tell me?

It was George Sampson who invented the first clothes drier
Sarah Boone - ironing board
I can't look "fly" if my clothes are jacked up

And what about my hair do?
The hair brush was invented by Lyda Newman
And the perm by Marjorie Stewart Joyner
All of this…I never knew
I never know that A. Miles - he made the Elevator
Biscuit cutter – Alexander Ashbourne
Lantern or lamp – MC Harney
The egg beater – Willis Johnson
Improvements to the guitar – make it like it sounds today –
Robert Flemmings, Jr.
Refrigerator – John Stanard
Bicycle frame – Isaac Johnson
And yes…traffic signal– Garrett Morgan

Why didn't they tell me?
then when I return home I can think M. V.B. Brown
for helping protect my home you see she invented the first
Home security system
A black female
You see that's how we get down

When I am tired and the baby gets heavy
It was William Richardson with the baby buggy to help me
carry…my baby

And what about J H Smith and the lawn sprinkler
Would there have ever been a slip and slide?
I think not…

Folks this is not
A coincidence
We should be proud of who we are
Because ….we are stars
And what about some summer fun
We owe – Mr. Lonnie Johnson for the invention of the super
soaker water gun
and just to help me stay cool
Alfred Cralle - who invented Ice cream scoop –
 I am now in my 30's so why am I just knowing
They deprived me of my childhood
And robbed me of my growing
Intellectually, mentally and socially.
My pride was not built
But rather they killed it
 It was like they meant for me to have this inferior mindset
And to be honest there were times when I felt even a little
regret
That I was black
Why is that?

You see this lack of knowledge
Crippled my growth
Damaged my self esteem
Made me even question my purpose for being here….
Of course now I know
But my children need to know
Your children do too
And this is just the first step

I am Woman...

And I am going to do all I can so that my children can know
Someone like me invented the toilet
It was JB Rhodes –
Bet you didn't know that?

And the sport they so long denied me
It was George Grant that invented the golf tee

All of this is my history
My black history
It's a part of me
And I am proud to be me
I'm proud of my history
I challenge you to
Get to know you
Who you really are
Even as slaves we were brilliant
We made up songs that had underlying codes
That told you where to go...
To gain your freedom
Do you hear me?
My people we are great
We really are kings and queens
Think about this
We are children of the true king
So with that mentality
we can do great things
we can be what we are destined to be
we can define our own identity
We are makers of many things
We are pursuers of our many dreams
We are imagination turned reality
We are leaders
We are teachers
We are believers
We are writers

We are survivors
We are presidents

Let's continue to build on this history
Let's continue to be a great part
Of history
Beautiful, Bold, Black, Great
With Greatness
You see
I am proud to be
A part of this history
I'm proud to be me
I AM BLACK HISTORY!

I AM BLACK HISTORY!

I am Woman…

I have been going to church for most of my life. I have lived in a few different states and so I have been to many different churches… different denominations also.

The next poem is about how I was feeling about some of them. The poem is not meant to offend anyone... I am simply sharing my feelings about my experiences in a church environment.

I sit and wonder...

What if God ...is truly unhappy?
...With the choir – and the songs they sing
Because they are not really ministering
It was all a performance and a show
Doesn't seem like they really want to go
Or even want you to go
To heaven

What if God
Looked down below
And saw that when there was supposed to be in prayer
That the children were talking and playing
And the parents don't even seem to care
About teaching them to be quiet and
Teaching them to let the words marinate
In their spirit
And then they wonder why
When they are older there is such a negative spirit
...In their homes

What if God
Saw that there are now
Male Preachers married to
Other male preachers
And they have a packed church
Not to discount the teachings as I have never heard them
before...and yes I know my sin is not better than their sin...
a sin is a sin....
But is that the message now...
Do what you want ...as long as you ask for forgiveness?
Is that now the norm?
Is that now what is acceptable?
Is that now the ONLY requirement to go to heaven?
Do what you want... Ask for forgiveness...get into heaven?

I am Woman…

What if God
Saw the lady that tried to fight me
In church last Sunday
Because her son was out of control
Kicking and whining and playing on his phone
When all I was trying to do was hear the sermon
He was acting like a 3 year old
But he was 12 ….And I simply asked him to stop
And it seems she forgot
where she was
She thought we were in a club
Cussing and screaming
Like I stole her man
It's hard for me to understand
Why just minutes later
She was up doing the "holy" dance

What if God
Saw the minister committing adultery… But teaching adultery
to be wrong
Then gets up on Sunday morning singing "He Saw the Best in
Me" song

What if God
saw the minister…That told the little girl to get off his stage
Because he felt she messed up his song
She was singing it all wrong
And no longer was allowed to be on the choir
And it didn't matter that her hearts desire
was to just give HIM praise…

What if God
Blessed my neighbor with the winning power ball
And she said she deserved it but refused to tithe at all

Because "if God wanted his 10% he would have given me more"

WOW!

What if God saw the phrase
Come as you are
Turn into daisy dukes
And no bra
Shouldn't there still be respect
To the children and elderly?
Or is it something to give the preacher to look at
Could it be?
Really?

What if GOD
Chooses not to forgive
Not to overlook
No more second chances
And says it loud and clear
That the lake of fire is in your very near
Future
What if he proclaimed ignorance is not an excuse…

Guess what
He was there
He saw it all
He heard it all
And He feels pain
And folks… IT IS NOT A GAME!

I am Woman...

Ever felt like you needed a vacation? You needed to just get away? The most important thing to remember is that you need to be able to know what or who you feel the need to get away from. Taking a vacation - many times – will only give you a temporary solution to a permanent problem. So I thought – what could be a permanent solution to the problems....
Aahh – the answer – DETOX!!

DETOX
I had to take a moment
Take a breather
From all the negativity
All the stress
All the things that were making me
Not be "me"

Poison can come in many forms
And what you do can make it seem normal

You have to be aware of what is hazardous to your health
What clouds your mind...
What keeps you awake at night...

You have to stop and think
Is there any other option?

Sometimes you just have to say "no"
It is a complete sentence you know.....
Sometimes you have to say "No" to the people and things that
you care most about

So if you didn't get a call back
Or I didn't return an email
Or comment on your post
Believe me it's not because I don't love you
Or I don't care
But I love ME.... more

Sometimes people can drain you
Take all of your joy
There comes a time when you have realize that you are worth
more
Especially when you do and do and do
More and more and then some more

I am Woman…

And they keep reverting back to the same mess that
Initiated the call in the first place

So I had to take a break
Take a breather
Because I am too important
God has so much in store for me
And I can't do what I am purposed to do
If I keep allowing you
To be that drug that is poison
To my mind
To my peace
To my sanity

It was hard
But I did what needed to be done
So I can continue to be
The one
To inspire
Motivate
Encourage
Not just others but myself too

It was hard
But I had to break free

I had to DETOX…

So I could get back to being… ME

Some of you may not have been to the place where the next poem will take you. So let me just explain... sometimes you want so hard to get acceptance from someone... and no matter how hard you try – you never really feel loved or cared for or that you even matter. Sometimes you have to pretend that the words don't hurt and the actions don't make you feel Irrelevant....

Sometimes you have to take a deep breath and say what is on your mind....

Here it goes!!!!

I am Woman…

I TRIED

I tried
to be the daughter the best daughter I could be
but it never seemed to be
enough for you

I tried to make you proud of me…
I paid for my own education -
Finally got my Bachelors - got to graduation -
And you made the celebration
A birthday party
for all those who had May birthdays in YOUR family -
You didn't understand that it was MY day -
And I needed you to say that you were proud of me ..
I needed you to say that even with all I had been through and
all the mistakes I had made -
That you were PROUD of me...
I didn't need for you to tell me I should share that day with
people who seemed to mean more to you that I did
Yes... I admit that I had the mindset of a kid
And even though… I was 32
I needed you
to be proud of me...

I tried to respect you
In the first book -
I published the poem I made for you when I was in 8th grade
I remember because that poem made
me proud that you were my mom
I was hoping you would look and see
that I had this desperate plea
to get "her" back
that even at almost 40 I still need my mother -

so when you come to my house and tell my son that he doesn't
need to respect me that I need to respect him and that the
conflict between me and him was my fault...
it hurts ...trying to respect you

I tried to be strong when my son tried to kill himself - and I
needed my mother - to take the time out to give me
encouragement and guidance and strength and hope - but
when he was in the hospital you felt it more
important to shop at BJ's than to come and support me and you
will never know how that made me feel...trying to respect
you...when you programmed him at an early age to call you
mom...I am trying to respect the fact that you lost your son and
I am not trying to have history repeat itself...but things are not
well the way they are...

I think about how you never took the time to get to know him
- 18 years...
that he was sick and didn't know and still doesn't know right
from wrong
and I was trying to show him love
even though I feel that you never showed me

You make it hard to respect you...
 now that he is 18 and you don't have my back and you don't
tell him that the streets are not the place for him.. that I have
instilled discipline, and overcome so much being a single
mother, and even lost "ME" a time or two - trying to do what
was best for him... to make sure he is not another statistic in
this cruel world...I needed you to have my back...

I tried to overlook the fact that you didn't give my daughter
anything for her birthday on becoming a teen- and the look on
her face when you decided to finally call a week later to tell
her that you would bring her something the next week but 3

I am Woman...

months later still nothing...and even on the day you called ...
instead of making the day be about her..
you told her how much someone else's child was growing and
what others were doing...

.. I tried not to cry - but my heart bled inside - trying to hide
the fact that now the feeling I was feeling all those years was
being passed on to my daughter -
and I want to make it stop - but the BIBLE says that I should
honor you.. so now I have this war on my shoulders - it's this
angel and this devil and they are in this constant battle and no
one seems to be winning... because
I'm trying to respect YOU ...

I tried to understand that even though - your relationships
were not model relationships they were all that I knew
so when my relationships turned - I needed you... to be the
one to tell me that I shouldn't look for love in a man who
doesn't understand the woman that I am and that he needed to
first hold my hand before grabbing my heart and tearing it
apart - that he should NEVER make me cry -
and if he did
then GOODBYE - was the best word... I could have said
 because the good means more than the bye
the good would continue to be birthed inside me
and the bye - would no longer tie me to someone who was not
meant for me...

I tried to understand...
I tried to forgive you...
all those times I wanted to talk to you but you didn't have
time...someone else was ALWAYS more important
they always trumped anything I could do or say
you seemed to have time to spend with me when I had money
...but when I lost my job because I am trying to make sure my

son stayed alive - and the money was gone - you disappeared
too.
I'm still trying to forgive you…

I tried to love you...
even when it seemed the love was not reciprocated
I hated the day you told me you never hugged me - because
you were not gay
so when my daughter comes to hug me or give me a kiss
I go out my way to make sure she doesn't feel like I did
I go out my way to show her that no matter how much she
may pluck my nerves
I never want her to look back and think I never loved her...
I do all that I can every day to show her... support her... and
tell her that I love her
and sometimes I pray that one day you will do that for me
too...
at least try to love me
the way
I try to love you...

I tried to hate you...
but simply can't...I can't hate someone who gave life to me
even though when I lost life - you didn't seem to care...
I remember when my dog died and I cried and cried - you told
me she was just a dog
but didn't hear me say that she was more than a dog she was
yet another child
that I don't have now and it seems you didn't care..
I can't lie - I didn't like you for what you said but couldn't
hate you...
I am now learning that even if I wished upon the biggest star...
I can't make anyone become who I want them to be ….
No matter how hard I've tried

I am Woman…

AND…even through it all
my heart won't let me stop
trying...

to be the daughter-
the best daughter I can be
because the hope still remains that one day it will be
enough for you!

I have not been in a relationship for over 7 years….
It's by choice of course and if you read the first book..
you would understand…

BUT…

Here is a thought….

I am Woman…

Beautiful!

I see his eyes – they smile at me
I see his smile – so inviting
Revitalizing – like a breath of fresh air
When I want to cry – he brings me joy and laughter and
Happiness
When I feel week – he picks me up and carries me
He tells me… everything is alright…
He gives me butterflies
He lets me
Exhale
He is …Strong …yet gentle
Protective
Caring
Loving
Encouraging
Honest
Respectful
Creative
Understanding
A friend…My best friend
He stimulates me… intellectually
He is emotionally stable
Willing and able
To make my believe in love again
Because he believes in fidelity
And he values family
Educated
Dedicated
Every night I see him in my dreams….and
I will know him when we meet …
Because …

He calls me Beautiful!

Work

January 12, 2015
I became Dr. Joy Lough
I successfully defended my dissertation....

Words cannot express that feeling I felt when it was all said and done
Overjoyed – you could say that...
But then I looked back and thought...

It had to be done
because
I lost my job trying to pursue it
Almost lost my child too
I lost family because of envy and jealousy
Didn't seem to be in the cards for me
Went through multiple mentors
And committee members too
Even had to change the method a total of 3 times
I will admit – I almost lost my mind
I can't remember how many nights I cried
Wanting to just give up
Because it was so hard...
And not having the support that I saw my classmates had
I felt bad.. and sad ... and even mad
At times
But I needed to continue
I needed to have something to show for it all

I have people that depend on me
I needed to be a warrior
A conqueror
A victor

I am Woman…

Because
Being a victim
Was not an option
I could not give in to defeat
When I speak to domestic violence victims
When I speak to the student that wants to give up
When I speak to the business person who is having second
thoughts
When I look into my child's eyes… I see
The reason for it all…
The reason this journey had to be
I feel proud to share my story…..

I do this for them….
I do this for you…
But mostly I do this for me….

And it is not over….
I still have so much more work to do….

Chapter 2: The Mother

I am Woman…

On being a mother….
I have been a single mother since day one for both of my
children. The journey has not been easy and when it is all said
and done – I would not change any of it for the entire world.

The first poem is a poem that my daughter and I recited at the
1st annual Mother-Daughter Dinner for the National Council
of Negro Women – Alamance Guilford Section.

That's why I love you!

J – my name is Joy and I have a daughter – a very lovely daughter…She has beauty inside and out and I wouldn't trade the world for her

M- my name is Mirakel.. I have a mother – a very lovely mother…She sees my beauty inside and out…She loves me like no other

J – we have some good days… We have some bad days...And we learn as we go

M – I know sometimes I don't make it easy…But I make it interesting that's for sure

J- she has a heart so pure…An innocence so new…Yet sometimes she acts so grown

M – She picks me up when I fall and never leaves me alone

J – with all my heart…I want what's best for you…I want the world to see the many gifts God has given you…And how very special you are to me

M – She knows to trust in GOD and teaches me to pray. She never gives up hope and she loves me every day

J – Do you know why Mirakel is your name? It's so the world will know the blessing that you are …And it's for me to be reminded - that my biggest miracle...Is anywhere you are….

M – and I am thankful God named you Joy…It's the perfect name for you…You always smile – you give me love…You think positive in everything you do…That's why I want to sing…That why I want to cheer…And I want to write

I am Woman…

poetry…just like you

J -Of all the daughters in the world

M - And of all the mothers too

(Together) - I'm glad to call you mine…That's why I love you

That Disease!!

I have no purpose
I don't want to live anymore
That's what he said
Then he walked by me and shook his head

What are you talking about?
That's what I said
And then he falls to the floor
What do I do?
What do I say?

Calling 911 but can't speak the words that
He took pills
Trying to take his life
Can't imagine why

Depression is what they call it
It can take your life before your live it
But Angels
God sent his angels
To watch over my son
It was the Angels that kept him alive
And angels that continue to do so

I pray
Every minute, every hour, every day
For him to get the healing he needs
And I'm praying we find a cure for
That disease

I am Woman…

Precious

When my son was nine
We found out that he had a brother who was also nine…
We know that every child needs a father
I grew up without mine and
I will be honest... there is a huge amount of resentment
I can't imagine what that means to other children
Especially a boy
But I am not going to let the fact of him choosing not to be
there to steal my son's joy

Still times were hard
Being a single parent was not easy
Not easy at all…in fact

Thanksgiving 2011 is a day I will never forget
My son tried to take his life
And with all that I have in me
I couldn't understand why
So I started feeling depressed
I started feeling hopeless
I started feeling helpless
I started feeling like a failure as a mother...

But God...

I know some of you may not believe
and it's not that I am trying to persuade you
or push my religion on you
But my God...

Placed angels around my baby
God placed angels around me

And I knew right then that I had to tell my story

There are avenues that I must use
I believe that God allowed this to happen
Because I need to minister to
Others going through
Or who have been though
What I have been through

I'm proud and thankful and just honored to say
That on June 7, 2013 - my son graduated
And on June 28th he saw his 18th birthday

You can't tell me that prayer doesn't work…
Because God knows I would not wish that kind of hurt
On anyone…
Not even on my enemies...

I am here to say
Cherish every moment of every day
Don't forget to say
The words… I Love You
Daily
And mean it…
And show it too

Say a kind word…
Even to a stranger
You never know
How powerful your words
Can be
And remember to
Smile… it really is contagious
Because
Life
Is
Precious!

I am Woman…

Chapter 3: The Friend!

I am Woman…

TO ENCOURAGE YOU!

The next set of poems are meant to be encouragement
No matter what you may be going through
Know that you …

Are Important!

What is your voice?
Listen to me…
There are so many choices of the voice that you can be
That you can choose to be
Or that you are
Think for a minute
When you look at me who do you see?
I am a female a black female
Ok ----so you say AND???
But when I speak….What do you hear?
I hope you hear determination preservation and joyfulness
I want you to hear kindness gentleness and genuine care
and joyful ness
When I speak… my goal is to tell you my story
To make you believe
To make you think
To make you realize
Possibilities
When I speak
My voice speaks on behalf of single mothers
My voice is of a daughter
And educator
An entrepreneur
A mentor
A writer
A friend
I speak of someone who has loved and lost
I speak of someone who looks back but not with regret –
she knows that
All of that HAD to happen
When I speak... I speak of dreams made reality
I speak of someone who has overcome adversity

So again I ask you…
What is your voice?
What are you saying?

I am Woman…

Are you telling your story?
Or someone else's
Are you living your dream?
Or someone else's?
Are you doing this for you?
Or someone else?
What is your voice?
When you speak...what do you want others to remember
What do you want them to say about you
Once you find your voice…
Then you need to put it to song
Add some instruments – some heart breaking heart
stopping - thought changing instruments
Find a beat – a beat that will make you dance slow or
break a sweat
Create harmony – with family, friends, loved ones – even
strangers
Make notes of inspiration
Comedy….of lessons…. of life
Sing of highs and lows
And brief moments of today
And of memories of yesterday
You can add a lot of happiness
Maybe even a little pain
And only a dash of fear
But when you hear
The finished product
WOW
When others hear
Your finished product WOW
Think about this ….your voice your song
You could change lives
You can inspire motivate
You can make history
And when you press rewind and then play again….
Remember you did it!

Breathe
You did it
You found your voice
 you made the choice
 to sing your song…
I encourage you to keep singing
But remember to start by finding your voice

I am Woman…

WHAT IS YOUR SONG?

What is your song?

There is a quote by Maya Angelou that says "A bird doesn't sing because it has an answer it sings because it has a song"

So I ask you again – what is your song?

What is your motivation – what's your mojo – what keeps you going what makes you know
What you wanna do
What makes you wanna grow
What makes you be you?

What is your song?

Is it love?
Is it family?
Is it money?
Is it just a feeling?
Or is it the prize that you know is at the end of it all?

What is your song?
I challenge you to find your song…
Find yourself
That's right find you….
Find your purpose
Find your dream
And make it come true
Find your song

Tell your story
Share who you are
Let the world know
Baby you are a star

Remember
It may be hard sometimes
Sometimes you may have to cry
There may be storms
The wind may blow
And you may have to start over

But don't give up
Don't let go
Remain focused
Because someone needs to know
Someone needs to hear
What you say
Someone needs to see
What it is you do

Someone may need you
To be their motivation
Be their inspiration
To be their light
Their guide
Show them the way

What is your song?

You may even need to just write your own song
Choose your instruments
But choose them wisely
Find your notes then make them flow
From lines to spaces and back again
– let them come alive on paper

In other words
Choose what you want to do
Choose the resources that are best for you

I am Woman…

Find the help the ones that share your dreams too
Find the ones that want to help your dreams come true
Then add a bit of you
Make the notes come alive on paper

What is your song?

Find your song
Make your song
And when you do
Sing it loud
Sing it proud
Even if off key
Even if you're a little bit pitchy
Be that bird
Sing your song
Don't you dare stop singing!!!

LISTEN TO MY SONG!!

Today I want to talk about my song…..
I looked in the dictionary and found the definition of a song to be: a short poem or other set of words set to music or meant to be sung:

I want you to…..Listen to my song
In order to listen to the song…it's going to take imagination and an open mind …..and I really need you to pay attention ….Are you ready…

Imagine…..The melody - I must tell you that the melody – represents… life, love, peace, happiness, joy, hopes and dreams… its beautiful and it's about us – you and me– can you hear it?

Do you hear the timing/ tempo it makes you
snap your fingers…pat your feet…move your body…

Tick tock tick tock
You know the timing in life sometimes fast or slow - ups and downs – highs and lows – we must have all of this in order to grow….

There is this combination of sharps – and flats – altos, sopranos bass and tenors - whole notes, half notes, quarter notes - again it's about you and me…do you see?

Can you feel the beat?

Now hear the drums – the heartbeat of my song – it's like my heart beat - your heart beat boom boom… can you hear it? again it's all the same so we should be on one accord –and in my song we are

I am Woman…

Taking deep breaths as we sing in - harmony in the verse and unison in the chorus –it's this collaboration –in this song that brings life

My song is like the keys on the piano black- white, ebony and ivory – you know like Stevie Wonder said – living in perfect harmony….
Yep that's my song – black, white, yellow, brown tan– all of us…coming together – all - together we're making this beautiful sound of friendship, trust, honesty – we are all in agreement, loyalty, respect and sincerity

Do you hear it?

Listen to the music - Soft and sweet and awe inspiring and unique
Motivating…
It's R & B, it's jazz, it's country….pop and rock and hip hop

Listen to the words- the language
The terminology
We all need to BE those words
It's then that you will see how we all connect and we all are one….
Because these lyrics are powerful

Are you listening?

Imagine if we all learned the words all the parts of the song
To the song
just think about this opportunity – to make a statement and change lives
with the words of my song … we do…
My song teaches the world to love and not hate
And it's for everyone… it doesn't discriminate
It picks you up when you feel down

It turns all frowns upside down
And sometimes you may cry – but trust me it's always tears of
joy
My song heals pain
My song feels greatness
My song message spreads love
And it shows forgiveness
It teaches patience
It delivers kindness
Yeah my song…

Just think how it would be when your friends sing it
when your family member sings it/ mom and dad and sister
and brother and boyfriend and girlfriend …. Imagine us all
singing …my song…
when you see people walking down the street headphones on ..
bobbing their heads singing my song – you feel what they feel
and it's all positive energy

how Beautiful it is … my song

so remember as you start your day and at the end of
day…even throughout the day …remember and sit in your
car…you can reflect on this day…take a deep breath and
..in your mind close your eyes ….just press play

and listen to my song ….

I am Woman…

Metamorphosis

Is defined as a major change in the appearance or character of someone or something

when I think of metamorphosis I think of butterflies….

Take the Egg…

Conception – it's not planned it just happened – so now we are here….

Caterpillar

Caterpillar: the larva. The Feeding Stage

We are feeding our brains – through knowledge and wisdom
that is gained
Through our school years and even through our tears
We fall off the bike – we learn to get back up
When the boy breaks my heart I learned to suck it up
I realized it was just a part of growing up

Pupa: The Transition Stage includes the cocoon

Experiencing the world we are big we are bad
– realizing that things weren't so bad at momma house
with no bills to pay -
you could just lay around
because momma protected you
just like that cocoon

Butterfly
Adult: The Reproductive Stage
Look at me –
I'm changing
Even as an egg
I was destined to be
More than I could have ever dreamed
You see
The caterpillar was not the end of my journey
No there was something inside that said
I am better than this
I am more than this
This does not define me
and I want you to know
No longer am I hiding in the cocoon - afraid to share
Afraid to dare
Afraid to be
Me

I am that black butterfly –

Unique - one of a kind

Exactly who I am

And my goal is to reach the hearts and minds

Of many

Through my words

I am trying to change lives

I want to be heard

And my first step

I am Woman…

Is to encourage you

Is to challenge you

To move into your

Metamorphosis

LISTEN TO MY VOICE……..
I want you to hear me…

I speak on behalf of single mothers
Because sometimes it gets hard
Working late nights, long hours
Going to school full time and still making time
For family
But I can't give up quitting is not an option
Not when you are so close to the finish
Not ever

I speak for the woman who has had her heart broken
Someone who has loved and lost
Someone who looks back and doesn't regret
She realizes that
All of that HAD to happen

I speak for the person who isn't ashamed to say
I messed up
I apologize
Please forgive me
And better yet – can you teach me to do better?

My voice is woman hood
But not from the hood
There is no…I wish a ****** would…
Making it happen
Making the dollar out of 15 cents
Yes I am telling my story
But I want to be captivating
Turning negativity into positivity

Proactive… creative

I am Woman…

      But what you don't hear
      What you won't hear
      Is negativity...
      Or "woe is me"
      Or poverty mentality
      You won't hear anything that is not me

      Are you listening?

      My voice is me
      And all that I have been through
      It is me
      So when I speak
      You hear my story

      What is your voice?

      What is your voice?
      What do you speak?

      When you hear me.. you feel my pain

      Even if you don't see me
      You hear me or you hear about me
      They say…
      "It's made her who she is now"

Tears of Joy
(Baby just cry)

Sometimes life can give you joy
Sometimes pain
Sometimes happiness
And even heartache
But hey… it's alright to cry

It's alright to cry
It's alright to shed those tears
Go ahead release your pain
Go ahead release your fears
I know you have some days
Some days you may feel weak
But know that those are the days
To help you reach your peak
There's joy in your life
In everything you do
It's the tears that you cry
That will help see you through
Whatever the problem may be
God is on your side
It's alright to cry
It's alright to cry sometimes

It's alright to cry
It's alright to cry sometimes
Because all of your pain
Will be healed over time
Just put your faith in God
Because he knows what's right
You may have pain through the day
But comfort overnight
Let the tears that you cry
Release your pain

I am Woman…

And let the pain that you're feeling
Let it go away
Understand that your life
Is so much more
Go ahead and cry
Your tears of Joy

Hey…
It's alright to cry
Crying tears can
Release your pain
And calm your fears
And hide your shame
You see tears can be
Joyful
Emotional
Resentful or even
Happy
What you feel inside sometimes you need to just
Let it go
Let it be
So you can grow
Into what God wants you to be
What He desires for you to be
And what I know you can be
Girls – Cry…
And then let him go if he's no good
And Guys – do what is right
You know that you should…
Cry - you can still be a man
And do what a man is supposed to do
I know that you can….

You see I cried
At my children's birth
I cried when the pain
Really hurt
When he broke my heart
And when I let him go
And when I had to start
Over…
I cried when I didn't know Him
I didn't know God
But now I know he is my peace
My joy
My Guide
 And yes I still cry
But more tears of joy
Than pain
And
It's really all up to you
Hey...
I'm just saying…

Tears of joy
Tears of pain
Tears of happiness
Tears of heartache

Chapter 4: To Be Continued...

The first book Tears of Joy: A Poetic Journey in the life of Ms. Joy - opened so many doors to so many opportunities...

It is with great JOY that I ask you to be on the lookout for future books from me that will focus specifically on...

*Domestic Violence Awareness
*Being a mother of a mentally ill child
*The Dissertation Journey
*Loving yourself – The self-esteem Series
*Get the Job! Tips on Resume Writing, Job Search strategies and the interview
*HR and your Small Business

I am Woman…

I am Woman

I am Woman…

www.ingramcontent.com/pod-product-compliance
Lightning Source LLC
Chambersburg PA
CBHW060419050426
42449CB00009B/2032